MAY 2015

Environment in Focus

Natural Wonders

Cheryl Jakab

Marshall Cavendish
Benchmark
New York

Website: www.marshallcavendish.us

This publication represents the opinions and views of the author based on Cheryl Jakab's personal experience, knowledge, and research. The information in this book serves as a general guide only. The author and publisher have used their best efforts in preparing this book and disclaim liability rising directly and indirectly from the use and application of this book.

Other Marshall Cavendish Offices:
Marshall Cavendish International (Asia) Private Limited, 1 New Industrial Road, Singapore 536196 • Marshall Cavendish International (Thailand) Co Ltd. 253 Asoke, 12th Flr, Sukhumvit 21 Road, Klongtoey Nua, Wattana, Bangkok 10110, Thailand • Marshall Cavendish (Malaysia) Sdn Bhd, Times Subang, Lot 46, Subang Hi-Tech Industrial Park, Batu Tiga, 40000 Shah Alam, Selangor Darul Ehsan, Malaysia

Marshall Cavendish is a trademark of Times Publishing Limited

All websites were available and accurate when this book was sent to press.

Library of Congress Cataloging-in-Publication Data

Jakab, Cheryl.
  Natural wonders / Cheryl Jakab.
    p. cm. — (Environment in focus)
  Summary: "Discusses the damage to natural wonders and how to best preserve them"—Provided by publisher.
  Includes index.
  ISBN 978-1-60870-092-9
  1. Nature conservation—Juvenile literature. 2. Environmental protection—Juvenile literature. I. Title.
  QH75.J347 2011
  333.72—dc22
                        2009042326

First published in 2010 by
MACMILLAN EDUCATION AUSTRALIA PTY LTD
15–19 Claremont Street, South Yarra 3141

Visit our website at www.macmillan.com.au or go directly to www.macmillanlibrary.com.au

Associated companies and representatives throughout the world.

Copyright © Cheryl Jakab 2010

Edited by Margaret Maher
Text and cover design by Cristina Neri, Canary Graphic Design
Page layout by Domenic Lauricella
Photo research by Sarah Johnson
Illustrations by Domenic Lauricella
Maps courtesy of Geo Atlas

Printed in the United States

Acknowledgments
The author and the publisher are grateful to the following for permission to reproduce copyright material:

Front cover photograph: Caves in Gunung Mulu National Park, © Tony Walthan/Jupiter Images

© Bob Krist/CORBIS, 28; © Galen Rowell/CORBIS, 16; © Paul A. Souders/CORBIS, 18; Image © J.Cunningham (1965), 21 (right); Image © R. Duffy (1999), 7 (top), 21 (left); Elphinstone Landcare group in Elphinstone, central Victoria. Photo: Elizabeth Mellick, 19; Charles Bowman/Getty Images, 5; National Geographic/Getty Images, 6 (top), 25; © Kristian Larsen/iStockphoto, 6 (bottom left), 9; © Tarzan9280/iStockphoto, 10; © Corbis/Jupiter Images, 6 (bottom right), 8, 13; © Thorsten Milse /Jupiter Images, 7 (bottom), 17; © Hemera Technologies /Jupiter Images, 24; © Tony Waltham /Jupiter Images, 23; Dave Fleetham/Pacific Stock/Photolibrary, 15; Adam Jones/Photo Researchers/ Photolibrary, 20, 26; © Wolfgang Amri/Shutterstock, 12; © Sebastien Burel/Shutterstock, 29; © capturefoto/Shutterstock, 11; © GagarinART/ Shutterstock, 27; © David V/Shutterstock, 22.

While every care has been taken to trace and acknowledge copyright, the publisher tenders their apologies for any accidental infringement where copyright has proved untraceable. Where the attempt has been unsuccessful, the publisher welcomes information that would redress the situation.

Please note
At the time of printing, the Internet addresses appearing in this book were correct. Owing to the dynamic nature of the Internet, however, we cannot guarantee that all these addresses will remain correct.

1 3 5 6 4 2

Contents

Glossary Words
When a word is printed in **bold**, you can look up its meaning in the Glossary on page 31.

Environment in Focus

Hi there! This is Earth speaking. Will you spare a moment to listen to me? I have some very important things to discuss.

We must focus on some urgent environmental problems! All living things depend on my environment, but the way you humans are living at the moment, I will not be able to keep looking after you.

The issues I am worried about are:

- large ecological footprints
- damage to natural wonders
- widespread pollution in the environment
- the release of **greenhouse gases** into the **atmosphere**
- poor management of waste
- environmental damage caused by food production

My challenge to you is to find a **sustainable** way of living. Read on to find out what people around the world are doing to try to help.

Fast Fact

Concerned people in local, national, and international groups are trying to understand how our way of life causes environmental problems. This important work helps us to learn how to live more sustainably now and in the future.

What's the Issue?
Natural Wonders in Danger

Today, some of the most spectacular natural wonders on Earth are in danger of being damaged by people. These sites are called natural heritage sites, and they urgently need protection.

What Are Natural Heritage Sites?

Natural heritage sites are places with significant natural value. They may contain important examples of:

- natural **biological features** or **geological features**
- threatened **habitats**, plants, or animal **species**
- natural areas of scientific, conservational, or **aesthetic value**

Protecting Natural Heritage

Natural heritage sites urgently need protection. Human populations across the world are spreading out into the remaining natural areas. Protecting these areas can prevent damage and loss of significant natural sites.

Heritage is what we get from the past and pass on to future generations. People of the future have a right to enjoy natural heritage sites, as we do today.

Fast Fact

In 1972, the United Nations Environmental, Scientific, and Cultural Organization (UNESCO) established the World Heritage Convention. This agreement protects heritage sites of significant value. These properties are added to the World Heritage List.

The Giant's Causeway, Ireland, is considered an important geological feature.

Natural Heritage Issues

The most urgent natural heritage issues around the globe include:

- tourism and **introduced pest species** endangering unique island species
- **overfishing** and **global warming** damaging coral reefs
- population pressures reducing land for wildlife
- rare and unusual habitats damaged by visitors
- geological sites damaged by tourism

N O R T H A M E R I C A

United States

N O R T H A T L A N T I C O C E A N

Caribbean Sea

Galapagos Islands

ISSUE 5

United States
Tourism is damaging the Grand Canyon. See pages 24–27.

ISSUE 1

Galapagos Islands
Rare species are being threatened by introduced pest species and tourism. See pages 8–11.

ISSUE 2

Caribbean Sea
Overfishing, pollution, and global warming are damaging coral reefs. See pages 12–15.

Around the Globe

Fast Fact

The first twelve World Heritage sites were listed in 1978. Some sites, such as the Galapagos Islands, were listed for their natural heritage. Others, such as the churches of Lalibela in Ethiopia, were listed for their cultural heritage. This is heritage created by the actions or cultures of people.

England

EUROPE

AFRICA

Democratic Republic of the Congo

NORTH

PACIFIC

Tropic of Cancer

OCEAN

Equator

INDIAN

OCEAN   AUSTRALIA

ISSUE 4

England
Formations in cave systems are being damaged by visitors. See pages 20–23.

ISSUE 3

Democratic Republic of the Congo
Wildlife and habitat in Virunga National Park are threatened by increasing human populations. See pages 16–19.

Island Species in Danger

Many islands have a great range of unique plants and animals. These are an important part of the world's natural heritage. However, many species of plants and animals found only on World Heritage-listed islands are **endangered**.

Biodiversity on Islands

Islands and the waters around them are rich in **biodiversity**. Although these areas make up only one-sixth of Earth's surface, they contain more than half of the world's sea life.

Threats to Island Life

Introduced pest species and tourism are the major threats to island **ecosystems**. They can damage habitats and disturb native animals. **Unsustainable development** and habitat destruction, such as clearing land for farms, also threaten island ecosystems.

Fast Fact

The most famous **extinction** of all was of an island bird species called the dodo. The dodo became extinct only about one hundred years after it was first seen by Europeans on the island of Mauritius.

The komodo dragon is an endangered species found only in the islands of Indonesia.

Many species on the Galapagos Islands, such as the small tree finch, live nowhere else on Earth.

CASE STUDY
The Galapagos Islands

The Galapagos Islands are very isolated islands in the Pacific Ocean, 621 miles (1,000 kilometers) off the coast of South America. In 1978 these islands became the first natural World Heritage site listed.

The Galapagos Islands are world famous for their biodiversity. There are rare species of birds and reptiles on each island.

Threats to the Islands

Tourism is the major threat to the Galapagos Islands today. The tourism industry has encouraged development and population growth, which means more land is cleared for housing and farming. Introduced pest species, such as goats, are also destroying the islands' habitats and biodiversity.

Fast Fact
The annual number of people visiting the Galapagos Islands increased from 40,000 in 1996 to 120,000 in 2007. The local population is increasing by 4 percent every year.

Toward a Sustainable Future: Valuing Island Systems

Today there is greater awareness that island systems are valuable. They contain a large part of the world's biological natural heritage.

List of World Heritage in Danger

The Galapagos Islands have been added to the List of World Heritage in Danger. This means that, unless there is an improvement in conservation, the site will lose its World Heritage listing. The list alerts the world to the need for action and gives the islands extra protection.

Global Island Partnership

In 2005, the Global Island Partnership was called for by the Seychelles and Palau. These island nations were urgently in need of assistance to protect their natural heritage. The Global Island Partnership led to the creation of a United Nations program to manage island biodiversity sustainably.

Fast Fact

Adding the Galapagos Islands to the List of World Heritage in Danger focused attention on damage from tourism. It also highlighted the need to change the way tourism is managed.

The Seychelles giant tortoise, part of the Seychelles' natural heritage, was thought to be extinct until 1997.

Habitat conservation on Madagascar helps protect many lemurs, including the ring-tailed lemur.

CASE STUDY

Conserving Madagascar's Rain Forests

Madagascar is an island off the coast of southeastern Africa. It has a rich variety of wildlife and up to 10,000 species of plants. The rain forests of Madagascar are now one of the highest conservation priorities in the world.

Extinctions on Madagascar

There have been many extinctions on Madagascar since the arrival of humans less than 2,000 years ago. They include a lemur the size of a gorilla, a pygmy hippo, the largest flightless bird in the world, and giant tortoises.

Conservation Efforts

In recent years Madagascar has become well-known for conservation efforts. These efforts focus on the habitat of lemurs. Black-and-white ruffed lemurs have been bred in captivity to increase their numbers. The first of these lemurs were released into the wild in 1997.

Coral Reefs Under Threat

Coral reefs are marine habitats formed by animals called coral polyps. Many of these reefs are now threatened by overfishing, pollution, and global warming.

Coral Habitats

The best-known reef-building coral polyps live in habitats of shallow, warm, tropical waters. Many animals and plants live in or around coral reefs, including species that are sources of food.

Fast Fact
The U.N.'s World Conservation Monitoring Center began mapping coral reefs in 1994. It has produced global maps of coral reefs in the World Atlas of Coral Reefs, available online.

Damage to Coral Reefs

Overfishing, pollution, and even mining are damaging coral reefs across the globe. Most coral polyps live in only a narrow range of temperatures. This puts reefs at risk of damage from global warming.

The damage to coral reefs threatens biodiversity and ecosystems around the reefs. The death of a reef destroys the habitat of plants and animals that live there. It also threatens people who depend on the reef for food.

Coral reefs are the habitat for thousands of species of animals and plants.

If the parrot fish population declines, the health of coral reefs will suffer.

CASE STUDY
Declining Coral Reefs

There has been a dramatic decline in the health of coral reefs in the Caribbean Sea over the last twenty-five years. Many corals have died.

Coral Damage

In the 1980s, reefs in the Caribbean were devastated by the near-extinction of a sea urchin. This urchin ate seaweed on the reefs, creating space for coral polyps to grow.

Parrot fish are now the only seaweed grazers on many Caribbean reefs. If parrot fish numbers drop due to overfishing, the seaweed will take over and coral polyps will die.

Coral Bleaching

Coral bleaching occurs when coral polyps are stressed. The polyps expel the colorful algae that live inside them and soon die. Between 1998 and 2004, there were five major bleaching events in the Caribbean. In 2005, a massive bleaching was followed by disease and coral death.

Fast Fact
Protecting living things in the open ocean is difficult. This is because whaling and fishing cannot easily be controlled in areas far from land.

Toward a Sustainable Future: Caring for Marine Heritage

Marine heritage areas close to land, including coral reefs, are now getting more attention. However, other marine areas also need protection.

Adding to Heritage Lists

About two hundred World Heritage sites are listed for their natural values. Of these, only thirty-one are protected for their marine biodiversity. In 2002, UNESCO began exploring ways to add more tropical coastal, marine, and small island ecosystems to the World Heritage List. Many areas were identified, but as of 2009 only four had been listed.

Other Marine Areas

Marine heritage areas away from coasts need protection, too. They are threatened by pollution, deep-sea mining, and fishing. All of the World Heritage listed marine areas today are close to land.

Fast Fact
The Exuma Cays Land and Sea Park in the Bahamas limits fishing, and commercial fishing is banned. The number of young coral polyps in this park is increasing.

This map shows the current marine World Heritage sites.

Glacier Bay
High Coast
St. Kilda
Natural System of Wrangel Island Reserve
EUROPE
ASIA
Cape Girolata, Cape Porto, Scandola Nature Reserve, and the Piana Calanches in Corsica
Shiretoko
NORTH AMERICA
Whale Sanctuary of El Vizcaino
Sian Ka'an
Belize Barrier Reef
Islands and Protected Areas of the Gulf of California
Desembarco del Granma National Park
Banc d'Arguin National Park
AFRICA
Tubbataha Reef Marine Park
Area de Conservación Guanacaste
Pitons Management Area
Cocos Island National Park
Ujung Kulon
East Rennell
Galapagos Islands
SOUTH AMERICA
Brazilian Atlantic Islands
Aldabra Atoll
Komodo National Park
Great Barrier Reef
Coiba National Park and its Special Zone of Marine Protection
Shark Bay
AUSTRALIA
Peninsula Valdes
Greater St. Lucia Wetland Park
Gough and Inaccessible Islands
Heard and McDonald Islands
Macquarie Island
New Zealand Sub-Antarctic Islands
ANTARCTICA

The Great Barrier Reef is the largest World Heritage site.

CASE STUDY

Managing the Great Barrier Reef

The Great Barrier Reef in Australia is the largest coral reef system in the world. It is more than 1,240 miles (2,000 km) long. The site is managed by the Great Barrier Reef Marine Park Authority (GBRMPA).

Protecting the Great Barrier Reef

The GBRMPA uses a system of zoning to protect the Great Barrier Reef. Different areas can be used for different purposes, such as general use, boating, fishing, and research. Some parts of the reef have full protection and may not be used for any of these purposes.

Reporting on the Reef

The GBRMPA must report regularly to the World Heritage Committee on the state of the reef. These reports are used to help plan the management of the Great Barrier Reef.

Fast Fact
In 1996 the Belize Barrier Reef Reserve System was granted World Heritage listing. It is the largest barrier reef in the Northern Hemisphere.

Wildlife Habitat Under Pressure

Some wildlife, such as large herd animals and **migratory birds**, need large areas of habitat. However, this habitat in deserts, forests, and **rangelands** is under pressure from people.

Land Habitat Under Threat in Africa

In the past, large areas of land in Africa provided habitat for huge numbers of animals. Today, these areas are being taken over by people.

Threats from People

The main threat comes from the rapidly increasing human population. Today there are so many people that competition for land is great. Animal habitat is often used for farming and building homes, particularly in areas where people are poor. Large land animals are also being hunted. Other threats from people include pollution, **poaching**, and unplanned construction.

Fast Fact

In 2007, UNESCO removed the Arabian Oryx Sanctuary in Oman from the World Heritage List. This was because Oman had not cared for the area. It was the first time a site had ever been deleted from the list.

African zebras and wildebeests need large areas of habitat to graze, but these areas are being reduced by increasing human populations.

Virunga National Park is one of only a few places where mountain gorillas can still be found.

CASE STUDY
Virunga National Park

Virunga National Park is in the Democratic Republic of the Congo. It contains the greatest diversity of habitats of any park in Africa. However, it is now threatened by increased numbers of people.

World Heritage in Danger

Virunga National Park was placed on the List of World Heritage in Danger in 1994, after a civil war in Rwanda. Millions of refugees came to the Democratic Republic of the Congo for safety.

The increase in refugees resulted in increased poaching and forest clearing in the park. People who were forced to leave their homes began to use the park habitat for their own needs. Forests were cut down for fuel, and thousands of hippopotamuses were killed. The gorillas that live in the park were threatened by loss of habitat and poaching.

Toward a Sustainable Future: Protecting Large Areas

Setting aside large areas as natural heritage sites is difficult when people are in need. However, it is a vital first step to saving many unique ecosystems across the world.

Importance of Large Areas

Large areas are important as habitats for large mammals and migratory birds on each continent. These animals depend on large expanses of land to survive. Because of this, they need protection from the pressure of increasing populations.

Protection from Rapid Population Growth

Many areas in Asia and Africa are threatened by rapid population growth. Large areas on each continent need to be protected for their natural heritage value. They can then be set aside before further development occurs.

Fast Fact

Two large-area sites were removed from the List of World Heritage in Danger in 2007. They were the Río Plátano Biosphere Reserve in Honduras and the Florida Everglades National Park. Each site has been improved, so they are no longer in danger.

Large mammals, such as moose, need large areas of habitat to provide them with enough food.

Recording protected vegetation helps people decide where conservation efforts, such as tree planting, are needed.

CASE STUDY

Connecting Country

Connecting Country is a large-area conservation project in Victoria, in southeastern Australia.

Biodiversity Crisis

Victoria is the most-cleared state in Australia. Few large areas of forests and grasslands remain. About a third of its native animals are either threatened or extinct. The native plants are in even worse condition. **Habitat fragmentation**, the spread of weeds, and introduced pest species have created an environmental crisis.

Recording Protected Vegetation

The Connecting Country project is recording areas of protected vegetation across central Victoria. This will create a computer database to show all private and public conservation areas.

Natural habitats in central Victoria are severely fragmented. Mapping conservation areas shows where there are gaps. This allows people to see where more conservation efforts are needed.

Threats to Hidden Areas

Many natural heritage areas are hidden underground, in jungles, and under oceans. These include cave systems, rare animal habitats, and deep-sea animal communities around **hydrothermal vents**.

Damage to Hidden Heritage

Many areas of hidden heritage are being damaged, sometimes before people even know what is there. Ocean floors, for example, are being mined and fished by damaging processes. Often, more damage is done by people when they find these hidden treasures. Sometimes the damage is deliberate. At other times it is simply careless, or due to large numbers of admiring visitors.

Cave Systems

Many cave systems have been added to the World Heritage List for their cultural and natural values. These values include geological features, natural beauty, biodiversity, and habitat for threatened species.

Some World Heritage Listed Caves		
Name	Country	Main heritage feature
Mammoth Cave	United States	Significant natural formations
Cave of Altamira	Spain	14,000-year-old cave paintings
Mogao Caves	China	Statues and wall paintings spanning 1,000 years of Buddhist art
Elephanta Caves	India	Rock art linked to the cult of Shiva
Naracoorte Caves	Australia	Complete fossil record

Ancient cave systems, such as Mammoth Cave in Kentucky, are popular tourist sites.

The Colonnades formation at Ease Gill had to be repaired after it was broken by a visitor.

The repaired column can now be seen by visitors.

CASE STUDY
Damage to the Ease Gill Cave System

The Ease Gill cave system in England has been named a Site of Special Scientific Interest because of its plants, animals, and geological features. However, carelessness and deliberate damage have had huge impacts on this important cave system.

Damage by Visitors

Some of the most spectacular formations in the cave system have been damaged by vandalism and careless or thoughtless visitors. This includes the Angel's Wing and Colonnades formations.

Preserving the Ease Gill Cave System

Preserving the natural heritage of the Ease Gill Cave System is important. The ancient rivers, stalagmites, and gravels in the cave system can give information about past climates. Tourism is welcomed to let the public connect with nature. However, it needs to be carefully controlled to avoid further damage.

Fast Fact
In 2006, a rock containing a 200-million-year-old fossilized dinosaur footprint was advertised on eBay. It had been stolen from Bendrick Rock, a protected site in Wales.

Toward a Sustainable Future: Sustainable Tourism

Tourism can bring important funds to support World Heritage sites, but it must be carefully managed to ensure it is sustainable.

Managing Tourism

Adding a site to the World Heritage List increases public awareness of the site and its values. However, the increase in tourists visiting the site needs to be carefully managed so the site is protected. In cave systems, this can be done by providing paths and erecting barriers. This limits the areas where tourists can walk. It can guide tourists through areas and reduce damage to the site.

Tourism can help local communities living in or near World Heritage sites, particularly in **developing countries**. It can provide jobs and bring money into the area. However, poorly managed tourism can do irreversible damage to heritage sites. Isolated and hidden sites are particularly open to damage, because guarding them can be costly.

Fragile cave systems can be protected from damage by the installation of pathways and fencing.

The number of visitors to the caves in Gunung Mulu National Park is limited to protect the site.

CASE STUDY

Gunung Mulu National Park

Gunung Mulu National Park is on the Pacific island of Borneo. It is famous for its cave systems. Transportation is improving in the area, so more people are able to visit the park. This has made the site vulnerable to damage.

Outstanding Heritage Features

Gunung Mulu National Park was given World Heritage listing in 2000. Its outstanding feature is the number of caves it contains. The cave called the Sarawak Chamber is the largest known cave chamber in the world.

Protecting the Site

World Heritage listing helps protect the site from the impacts of visitors. It assists in getting donations to pay for conservation. It also limits the legal use of sites. This means the number of visitors is limited to prevent damage.

Fast Fact
The Jeju volcanic island and lava tubes in Korea were named a World Heritage site in 2007. They are described as the finest lava tube system of caves in the world.

Protecting Geological Sites

Geological sites include places where landscapes created by erosion, volcanic activity, and **glaciers** can be seen. They also include sites containing fossils. Today, many of the most spectacular geological sites on Earth need protection from the impacts of tourism. Tour operators organize tours so visitors can experience these wonders of nature. However, some operators run tours that damage the very environment tourists are interested in visiting.

Damage to Geological Sites

Fast Fact

For at least 500,000 years the Naracoorte Caves in South Australia trapped animals that fell into them. In 1994 they were given World Heritage listing for their complete fossil record.

Rocks are hard and appear difficult to damage. However, poorly run tourism can cause damage and reduce the heritage value of sites. This damage can be permanent, such as the impact of thousands of people walking on tracks. It can also be something that makes a visit to the site less enjoyable for others. For example, noisy vehicles can disturb the environment.

Dinosaur Provincial Park, in Canada, is an important geological site that contains fossils that are 75 million years old.

Many people like to take flights over the Grand Canyon, but noise from planes disturbs other visitors.

CASE STUDY
Noise in the Grand Canyon

Noise from tourism is damaging the Grand Canyon in Arizona. The Grand Canyon is one of the most well-known geological World Heritage sites.

The Grand Canyon

The Grand Canyon has been carved out by the Colorado River over thousands of years. It is nearly 4,920 feet (1,500 meters) deep. The natural quiet in the canyon is astounding. Many people believe this is an important part of visiting the canyon.

Noise in the Grand Canyon

Today, the silence is gone. Instead, the noise of tourist flights fills the canyon. In 1987, the government passed a law to restore natural quiet to the park. On Earth Day in 1996, President Bill Clinton ordered a limit on the number of sightseeing airplanes. However, flights over and through the canyon continue to increase, as does the noise.

Fast Fact
The sides of the Grand Canyon contain layers of colored rock. These layers expose the **geological history** of the site for the past 2 billion years.

Toward a Sustainable Future: Ongoing Protection

Protecting world heritage, including geological sites, is an ongoing process. It is supported by the United Nations and many groups across the world.

Protecting World Heritage

The Convention Concerning the Protection of World Cultural and Natural Heritage protects World Heritage sites, such as the Grand Canyon. Under this convention, countries must inform UNESCO of any threats to their World Heritage sites. Threats include noise and visual pollution, as well as more direct physical damage or destruction of sites.

Balanced Heritage Listing

In its first twenty years the World Heritage List lacked balance. Of the 410 sites, only 90 were natural. Most were located in **developed countries**. In 1994, the World Heritage Committee began trying to fix this problem. Natural and geological sites across all parts of the world are now being listed.

Fast Fact

The World Heritage fossil sites of Sterkfontein, Swartkrans, and Kromdraai in South Africa are part of the "Cradle of Humankind." Remains of some of the earliest human ancestors are preserved at these sites.

Rangers at heritage sites, such as Mammoth Cave, can check to make sure the site is not being damaged.

Cruise-boat tours are now limited in Geirangerfjord and Nærøyfjord.

CASE STUDY

World Heritage Listed Fjord Formations

Fjords are deep valleys, cut by glaciers, that have filled with seawater. Two of Norway's most scenic fjords, Geirangerfjord and Nærøyfjord, were added to the World Heritage List in 2005.

Geirangerfjord and Nærøyfjord

Geirangerfjord and Nærøyfjord are two of the world's longest and deepest fjords. They are 75 miles (120 km) apart and are separated by the Jostedal Glacier. They were the first heritage sites in Norway chosen for their natural and geological value.

A Popular Place to Visit

The Geirangerfjord and Nærøyfjord areas are very popular with tourists. They are considered to be among the most scenic fjord areas on the planet. Heritage listing focuses attention on the need to control tourism, particularly the noise from cruise ships traveling up the fjords. Listing as a World Heritage site means tourism is more strictly controlled.

Fast Fact
Due to concern about global warming, some environmental campaigners want Mount Everest placed on the List of World Heritage in Danger.

27

What Can You Do?
Learn About Sustainable Tourism

Much of the damage done by tourists is due to lack of knowledge. When you visit a site, make sure you learn about sustainable tourism. This means making sure your travel will support the local community and will not harm the site.

Create Rules for Sustainable Tourism

Use the list below to help you create your own rules for sustainable tourism. Look at tourist brochures advertising a heritage site you would like to visit. Evaluate the tours using your list, to see if they support sustainable tourism.

Sustainable Tourism Rules

- Inform yourself of the environmental impacts of your visits.
- Learn about the heritage value of the sites you are visiting.
- Travel outside the peak seasons to avoid overcrowding.
- Use local guides and accommodations that return profits to the community.
- Show respect for local cultural heritage and the environment.
- Buy local products and pay a fair price to producers.
- Visit local sites that conserve nature and culture.

Many heritage areas have information centers where you can learn about the site you are visiting.

You can study the natural heritage of your local area or a World Heritage site near your home.

Create a Tourist Brochure

Each area has distinct cultural and natural heritage. Create a tourist brochure for a World Heritage site in your local area, state, or country. Advertise the special features that make it (or could make it) of world heritage value. These may be geological, biological, or cultural heritage features. The example below focuses on geological and landscape heritage.

Geological and Landscape Heritage

Make a list of the major geological or landscape features in your chosen area. Think about the following information for your brochure:

- What mountains, volcanoes, gorges, rock formations, or other features are of interest?
- How big are these compared to others in World Heritage areas?
- What types of rocks are there?
- How can you find out how old these rocks are and how they formed?

Fast Fact
The United Nations Heritage Convention describes heritage as both cultural and natural. This is to remind people that it is important to maintain a balance between humans and nature.

Toward a Sustainable Future

Well, I hope you now see that if you take up my challenge your world will be a better place. There are many ways to work toward a sustainable future. Imagine a world with:

- a sustainable ecological footprint
- places of natural heritage protected for the future
- no more environmental pollution
- less greenhouse gas in the air, reducing global warming
- zero waste and efficient use of resources
- a secure food supply for all

This is what you can achieve if you work together with my natural systems.

We must work together to live sustainably. That will mean a better environment and a better life for all living things on Earth, now and in the future.

Websites

For further information on natural heritage, visit the following websites.

- Our Place: The World Heritage Collection
  www.ourplaceworldheritage.com/index.cfm?&action=ourplace
- United Nations Environment Programme World Conservation Monitoring Center www.unep-wcmc.org/index.html
- UNESCO photo bank http://photobank.unesco.org/exec/index.htm
- Earth Science World Image Bank www.earthscienceworld.org/images/

Glossary

aesthetic value
The value placed on a site for its beauty.

atmosphere
The layers of gases surrounding Earth.

biodiversity
The range of living things in an area.

biological features
The living things that are significant or typical in an area.

cave systems
Complexes of large, connected caves or holes in the ground.

developed countries
Countries with industrial development, a strong economy, and a high standard of living.

developing countries
Countries with less developed industry, a poor economy, and a lower standard of living.

ecosystems
All the living and nonliving things in an area, and their connections with each other.

endangered
At a high likelihood of becoming extinct.

extinction
Loss of a species when all its members die out.

geological features
Landscape features made up of rocks and soil.

geological history
The history of the rocks and other geological features of an area.

glaciers
Huge blocks of moving ice.

global warming
An increase in the average temperature on Earth.

greenhouse gases
Gases that help trap heat in Earth's atmosphere.

habitat fragmentation
Breaking up large areas of habitat into smaller areas, for example by clearing parts of a forest.

habitats
The areas used by living things to provide for their needs.

hydrothermal vents
Cracks in Earth's surface underneath the sea, where the water is warmed by the heat inside Earth.

introduced pest species
A non-native species that damages the environment.

migratory birds
Birds that live in different regions during different seasons.

overfishing
Taking too many fish from one area or species, leading to a decrease in numbers.

poaching
Taking or killing wildlife illegally.

rangelands
Broad areas of land used by grazing animals; can be made up of grasslands, forests, and scrublands.

species
Living things of the same type that can reproduce.

sustainable
Does not use more resources than Earth can regenerate.

threatened species
A species that is likely to become endangered.

unsustainable development
Developing industry, tourism, and standards of living in a way that uses more resources than Earth can regenerate.

Index